OVERLAND

Also by **NATALIE EILBERT**

Indictus

Swan Feast

OVERLAND
NATALIE EILBERT

Copper Canyon Press
Port Townsend, Washington

Cover artwork: Mary Hark, *Driftless Reveries,* 2010. Handmade flax and abaca paper, indigo dye, mixed media, 29 × 25 inches

Cover design: Becca Fox Design

Copper Canyon Press is in residence at Fort Worden State Park in Port Townsend, Washington, under the auspices of Centrum. Centrum is a gathering place for artists and creative thinkers from around the world, students of all ages and backgrounds, and audiences seeking extraordinary cultural enrichment.

The Library of Congress has catalogued this record under LCCN 2022046795.

9 8 7 6 5 4 3 2 FIRST PRINTING

COPPER CANYON PRESS
Post Office Box 271
Port Townsend, Washington 98368
www.coppercanyonpress.org

JUL 1 8 2023

For those who could not survive

Landscapes are radical tools for decentering human hubris. Landscapes are not backdrops for historical action: they are themselves active.

Anna Lowenhaupt Tsing

*Heaven- and earth-
acid flowed together.
The time-
reckoning worked out, without remainder.*

Paul Celan

I knew the two hungers

*One licks the sugar
The other holds the bowl*

Matthew Henriksen

CONTENTS

I

5 Overland
6 In Situ Adaptation
7 Transverse Orientation
8 (Earth), the
9 Mediastinum
11 Natalie Eilbert, by User 4357
12 Kolumbo, 1650
14 The Sun Is Shining
15 The Lake
16 Intercourse
17 Green Bay, Wisconsin
18 Stop
20 There Is Hope

II

23 Caliche
24 Surge
26 Land of Sweet Waters
27 Consultation
28 Edge Habitat
30 The Lake
31 Bacterium
33 Gunmetal Gray
34 Eat and Keep
35 Bone
36 If Each Day I Lose Momentum
38 The Lake
44 Imaginal Discs

III

49 Crescent Moons
51 The Ritual
52 Malignant
55 It's a Girl!
57 Do Not Intervene
58 Psalm for the World Below

61 The Lake
68 Chippewa Falls
69 Virgin Psalm

IV

73 Three of Swords
75 Wet Season
76 Fieldwork
77 White Noise
78 Cougar Kill
79 They Do Not Eat Until They Cleanse Themselves
80 For Seth
81 Earth (the)
82 The Lake
93 The Limits of What We Can Do

95 *Acknowledgments*
97 *Notes*
99 *About the Author*

OVERLAND

OVERLAND

It isn't useful to celebrate being alive.
But I'd like to be generous. Of the hand
that feeds, look to the carpals,
a mechanism that takes until it spoils.
Of the fruit, I bite into its resource,
the orchard harvester's bee stings. I bite
into its lesions, the hard skin of poverty
so far removed it isn't even the hand biting
the hand. Bravery feels so industrial.
What would they think of my survival?
To pan out is to spot the moldering fountain
tumored with brown coins. I cannot look again.
So I awaken to multivitamins, piss
a healthy neon. I wash a knife, its
blade a good worker. I eat an apple,
an orchard firmed by capital. At the store
I pay extra for organic, the buck twenty that could
keep a village fed for a week, the payment
a wish to clear my name. Of the water,
it sputters bacterially from a fountain. What
should I tell my three-month nephew
about the gunmetal ocean, his name also Gray.
Should I tell him about all the clucking fathers
who said *Not in my lifetime,* a phrase that raised me
tender and plump? A duck
sleeps on cement, its head curled under
a wing. Beyond, a lake, a discourse. Blue
matter of a life I couldn't refuse. The wind,
a catalogue of known things, parts her feathers.

IN SITU ADAPTATION

At the climate change rally, I follow the teens, and no, I am not thinking
      about the nine-inch sea level rise in New York since 1950,

topsoil erosion along Midwestern farmlands, the rills, gullies, and streams
      that pour into a hypoxic Gulf, every short clip of annihilation

like a cold hand on the back soothing a cigarette burn. All these rolling
      hills flattening under black vertical weather, always already inescapable.

I am thinking my body can barricade, can be rows and columns of eyes
      like a vigilant Eden amid her beings. When the daisy chains and zip

ties come, the teenagers know to ball their apprehended fists
      for the brief allowance of room in the hard carceral lines

cinched at the wrists. One day, this pain, a consonant pinching skin,
      will deaden the waters forever. Every mass arrest is plastic, a future of

waste to choke on. The teenagers chant the song of dissent and I clench
      and unclench the fantasy of a filled womb, the wet knot of never

as I cool against a Bank of America tower. And it's true I shouldn't
      say *never,* but it enters me like a filthy gulp of lake water

as I sink three versions of me down. The crowd is a jawline stroked
      in quiet moments, plasticking elsewhere as I dizzy in image

stations: stomped grasses in the greenway, a surface of earth that agrees
      to sludge and lilies, lead and benzene, beer spit and Whitman.

O—, the devastated watersheds, the dream of a child, and I knew I knew
      a bloom / a hyacinth / an oxygenation. Winds disperse every species into

cold land and hot land and I was so close to each day picking eyelashes from a
      face on clean linens. This is what I tell myself: Even here, at

the end of all, I stayed in the lake at the bottom of my loneliness.

TRANSVERSE ORIENTATION

A fire begins from the hands. A filament rings with incandescence
—not poetry strictly, a lightbulb shaped as bodice. Moths navigate air

guided by the moon. Body positioned to gravid North Star. The department
secretary says *North Star* to suggest there is hope despite obstacles. I

write "North Star" with follow-up bullet points. Animals fixate on primeval
paths. Migratory path. Moon path. Magnetic-field path. Tremor path.

They walk impossible interstates and die. They fly into fire moons and die.
They snap into blue and die. Dark waters absorb heat and they die. They die.

I never pled with the moon to save me. I set my arm on fire with hair spray.
I closed my eyes to the highway and stepped into her dark waters. I sipped

pebbles one two three and slept for miles, an administrative moon driving
moths and waves and wombs and each glib cliché. We see the moths

fried to the bottom of bulbs as a lesson in pleasure, punishable by death.
And look at us, guided by similar light—that you would have me change.

(EARTH), THE

Oh, problems, I've never
      been resilient anyway. The ropes
eventually biodegrade around
      my wrists. *Phosphor* is a pretty
pretty word, even as it modifies
      runoff. When I tell academics
we've entered a threshold without
      bugs, they laugh and say I should
come to the South and say that. It's like the
      senator who brought a snowball to Congress;
together we walk into private conveniences.
      What we do is we spend us. I am not empty
of metaphor; I am tired of multitudes.
      The indelible crush of leaves. Grass
upturned in battle for the ball. Gravel,
      gravel. Animals grow bigger at the end
of their epoch. The wind soothes only
      when we need confirmation. Close
your eyes to breeze. I am not the promise
      of forgetting. I merged regretfully
and I, too, missed the point. No tonnage,
      no respirators. No Edenic twist.
O chronic, heavenless now. Look—
      a scorch mark in California lumber
resembles the tilted shape of Saturn, the
      pretty pretty rings of disaster, crashed
moon cores why I'm done with
      landscapes. Below this beauty,
nothing lives. Disaster—my hands shake with
      its white vantage. Oh, problems,
my plastic movable cunt, *disaster* a word loved
      by what comes after, and we
without stars, our bodies alive, thickened—

MEDIASTINUM

I thought very hard and thought of nothing.
Jesse Ball, *Census*

In one segment of the landscape, a hyena drags her clitoris
across the plains, a dust perfuming up. Cicadas pulse the segment,

a femur filled with rain. It is a lush grassland within which
the greens have sprouted through the exposed joints of animals.

This seems to be a metaphor for growth and resistance. A
single, singed dollar rolls through the wind. I read

a book that imagines, among other things, a world without
trees. I wrote a book that imagines, among other things, a world

with trauma only. The book splayed facedown on my parents' dresser,
to an early part of the book. People do this when they no longer

want to see information. I no longer want to see information.
In another segment, a series of weasel-oil candles—such is

the cure-all in this aspect of land. Mostly the candles are not
lit. At night the moon makes the earth shine like bottle

flies, a glimmer here and there where a lachrymose flame
continues on. A god peeks past the clit of the hyena

disapprovingly, as evidenced by their glare and nod. But I
want a god to glare and nod. I want a god to do anything at all

with my debts. In another segment, my grandmother
lives, and she watches a pack of lionesses feasting inside

the rib cage of a zebra. At first, she tells us, she believes
the zebra to be breathing in sleep, but the lions move

her chest beneath the membrane of bones.
It's like I always say: The evenings wait for the kind of

death we get, and we are so very fond of the evenings.
In another segment, the last one, we know it to be last

because a single woman is braiding her hair in a desert.
We have been here before. An animal raises her leg.

NATALIE EILBERT, BY USER 4357

There's there there. A sweet, empty
vacuum bag smells of industry,
a provenance. I try a xylophone
note, a sound like burnt yellow.
Approximations don't
mimic; they stand
in a room
full of doors. My legs
are hungry for money,
hang over a man's ribs.
I argue I am trying to be myself
when I sever a cucumber. Each
object presents its presiding objects.
An elbow grinds
into a caramelizing thigh bruise.
I remove an article, an
article too particular to understand.
A kitten sleeps, shaped
as a pair of slumped lungs.
I must laugh at my brain fog,
saran wrap over my eyes.
Is authorship anything? I am a
single combination of cells,
dander under a god nail,
duplicating. I press my thumb
to my femoral nerve until
a white light blinks myself open.
I enter me, a door warped.
In the crease, there.

KOLUMBO, 1650

It wasn't wind. It differently burned.
My child's child, a reptile in pumice. A white
that wasn't a cloud. Santorini, a blown
gasket, disappearing into a future without us.
I had no skin. So many nights, I held my wrist
over coal to cauterize the open veins. To

not die, you see, was a powerful choice. To
every morning, this was all to life there was. Burned
and hostile, I wasn't ready to unhook from your wrist.
A wave and then another. Islands flanked with white.
I among the seventy-plus lost to the caldera. Among us
I lived least on a trajectory. A lit, wet stick blown

shut. My body? It finally shut, and me? the gases blown
up and gone, a decay that tastes azure blue. To
the charred donkey, pleasure in the gaping ribs, us
usurped of equine dust. It wasn't for you I burned
and it wasn't for anyone. Santorini, a white
knuckle of rocks, empty hands, empty wrist.

The slump of cats and dogs, fur curled at the wrist.
Pyroclastic flow, the process of gas and matter blown
along the ground. It wasn't wind but a bursting white
beneath us. I watched my neighbor launch up and to
an anticlimactic land, a body there a body burned.
We smelled the orchids in her arms, she was so close to us.

First my blood evaporated. No, it was crude rust for us,
not like the great ants I tried to stomp inside my wrist
when I was young. And I married. That meant I burned
to watch him anywhere. Kolumbo, a line of twenty blown
and unblown volcanic cones, I wished I could fasten to
anyone. To be dead and still as a tsunami triggers into white

shadow above us. That's love for you, a terror so white
it cleaves the bones. My brain evaporated next to us.
It was so hot and dry and chemical. How dull it was to
be in our Bronze Age, weaponized down to our wrist
and still to be decimated. And still to be heated up, blown
like a wave in the Aegean. My ligaments detached, burned

as only snow can burn the wrist. A wave and then
another blown. I see only snow. An orchid grows along my iliac
crest. To us, it was a white melody, a white rust, is white.

THE SUN IS SHINING

A freight train exhales a distant era I've never known
as a skinny squirrel scavenges my driveway. It keeps being
the day again. The weather so goddamn pleasant. Roofers
hammer at a forty-five-degree angle and I attempt to locate
unnameable birds that shape the trees with their chirps.
I have always wanted to die. A robin hops along the leaves
and I google, *do birds have knees?* I have exhausted my
presence again. That I am someone else's warm body, I can
only laugh. After my father passed out in the kitchen,
he reported his wife calling his name from the top of a well.
When my mother watched her husband faint, she shook
in her new knees, her sutures still scarring. His irises drained
of color, she told me. My brother coughs and wheezes elsewhere
for air. I touch my cheek and close my eyes. Dowdy life pushes through.

THE LAKE

I've forgotten how to live. A new release
          of *Blair Witch Project*
reminds me. Smoke pours from a window, night a green
       mouth. I spoon berries under my tongue, miss

the private faith in restriction. From a screen,

I watch, smoke pours from a window, night a green
       mouth. My brothers have turned libertarian all of a sudden,

          all night my mind bleeds through a screen, what
are your policies, what are your policies, what are.

      What doesn't appear in the news, the cops in their
      cars rolling up to Black neighborhoods, whoop of the sirens.
      Authorities who look for a reason to shoot is a crime that should
      air twenty-four seven. This is not in the news.

      I watch in real time
a car back up into a building. I remain safe. I've forgotten how

      to live. I'm gifted garden tomatoes, a zucchini.
Lie with Notley in bed, know I am not

      disrupting a void. The divine question of love,

when love ends we are forced to begin. *Begin and cease——*

INTERCOURSE

In the dream, someone betrays me or I am betrayed. I want
to be the woman bereft and clutching her dearest keepsake.
I have no memories, no altars. For heirlooms I have rayon
and shredded cotton from H&M, one pilled sweater. A mother

never braided my hair into black stations. Instead, a landscape swells
with creatures, a rotten tumor in an ambling quadruped's joint.
A carriage of organs bound tightly by cerulean film. I love as if
nobody can betray me, like I'm a girl emptied of values, a dumb

malignant seed in a cab to the airport, a flat fee, a hand up the
thigh of a buckled lap. In a decade, I am a landscape only. I hold
asanas to release my hamstrings, an area, I'm told, where we store
our grief. Where in our body is not grief? Time tires us out. This

is why we invented it, so we might form from ends. I roll lactic
bubbles under my face with rose quartz, fuck a pillow in sleep.
In my body I am not alive. I am weather in a landscape, juiced
blue films, pockets of tangy heat, blood networks like an internet

returning to epicenter. Shit, acid, nitrates. Gurgles miraculous.
I dream in a lonely passage of sodium and potassium blinking
open. Chains of work without rhetoric or pasture or gravity or love.
I consider some last questions. A factory blooms. Would I die without you?

GREEN BAY, WISCONSIN

How did I end up in Richard Scarry's universe?
Polychlorinated biphenyls filled the river
for thirty years and I read a new life study,
the social determinants of health, incidence rates.

Against all odds I am the portrait of health.

I pay for monthly Patreon subscriptions to hold asanas
and I've held my stomach in since age ten.

The monsters inside me are only organs
absorbing carcinogens. The sky a colorful sarcoma
under which all beings die. I told myself

a story that fills me with batting, makes me
an incendiary material derived in a factory, makes me
liquid waste dumped in the earth to contort
a future in utero. The waste inside is useful. Every day

the scientists cite numbers as I check my negative
balance. I request payment from a grant that wants me
to live, from a government that can't save its future.

I prewrite a story on election results. I write
"in an election with historically low turnout." I write
"[blank] won in a landslide." A landslide.

STOP

I can never distinguish Kafka stories.
          Someone locks their car?
The Metra pushes
      through atmosphere? Being at a tower?
                  A guard
who denies entry? A cold case isn't solved and a man outside,

he is singing. I miss the smell of a torso. The armpit hair's

animal salt. A click in the wall. The smell of a torso. Your. My family

gasps for air beneath a township. A shutting
                      door. The neighbor

        climbs up her stairs, not hers.
I drag the ball of my foot across a loose

floorboard nail. It hurts enough. Your voice an idea nasaled through.

I twirl my hair. The cat places down your tie. Kitten teeth scatter
like fingernail clippings piercing skin.
              I smooth down my gown as I sit. There,
a space of no tenderness. A body hovering down to surface, strong quads

the YouTube yogi gifted them. A veil,
             I have never touched one. An orange releases
its ambers. The word *guillotine,* a guilt, an orange released. She blows

a dandelion, story in reverse. A truck screeches. Grass stains, a twisted knee.

She asks me at two in the morning if I've ever, *you know.*

          Once, I lie. I spit up a bottle of pills. Flush them
into a fragile watershed. Oh, my endocrine-disrupting compounds, the poor
    growth of aquatic life

and my fear of centuries. She asks if I am safe. The whale song of freighters wafts an indistinguishable distance from here.

THERE IS HOPE

I have settled into myself. A sediment no longer clouds
up in liquid bloom. In stillness, I see my particulates.

I don't know if it's the same for you. M tells me no one
should be able to undermine my power, but isn't power

drawn from the threat of being overthrown? Take
this bridge. Men engineered a line over water to connect

two futures. I walk a bridge toward a future so slowly,
a wisteria tracing the air for animal warmth. I no longer

want to be animal warmth. Rarely does a bridge collapse.
Pedestrians walk with purpose across time, from one

future to another. We line up for our loneliness here,
alone, alive, to see the spectacle of it. The shine of sun

over the surface of a river. Rarely do jumpers die
from drowning. The water is a splitting surface. The fall

another line connecting futures. The body stops at
seventy-five miles per hour, the organs jolt forward and sever.

A man wrapped in soiled blankets sleeps, two dots
and a line slacking futures. The sun shines over the river.

On impact, the ribs break. The surface as hard as the past
we cannot fix. I could have loved you fiercely.

CALICHE

I don't know how many ways a body can end.
Night is a steady calculus, volitional in its
grief. What was resolved in all these books on
poisoned water and child cancer yielded no
causation. Girls die from a knot behind the
spine one after the other and this is a confidence
interval. Page after page, the fanning of money.
Inside a book, the decades-old action group
ends contorted. I pull a 1968 *Life* magazine
from its sleeve and read the anger back into
hippies. Only one agitator in the Dakota crowd
to greet Nixon, thrown from the rally in a
familiar way. The Santa Barbara oil spill, the
neglect at San Miguel, dead, slick pups between
rocks. Disappearance is active loss. We lose
the world with deliberate focus. Factory dyes
bleed into spongy soil for two world wars.
Neuroblastoma mutates in utero, cancers primed
for footnotes. I think about what of us medical tools
shave off: my uncle's squamous cell carcinoma, four
joints of my mother, the remnants of a brother.
San Miguel's centuries-old root systems remain
in a calcium-carbonate cast, the vegetation gone.
Tourists call this a forest but it looks a statuary
of Marys praying every direction for a relief
that cannot come. We can say the sun drenches
Earth with gold. All day, we can say this.

SURGE

Invasion is not a metaphor for the virus,
and it is not how my country invades. I open
a window to let weather in. A river nearby

flows over weather as weather invades
weather. It is not a metaphor for rain but
how one can be entrapped by the fist

of another. Quarantine, named for the
forty days alone, thought to cure us, Jesus

who fasted forty days in the desert. Jesus
I've been hit so hard my ears rang over

the broken pinky bone all night. Alone
with the fist on one side of life, a bug on
the other. Water runs faster over smooth

plastic than rough stone, never mind the
one part per billion trimers. Man makes
the weather a race to beat while time has

made me scared. An invisible thumb on
my trachea, a wrench in my skull. I slide

my fingers past my waistband to the cliff edge
beneath I call I. I move my fingers to the

optimism of the lake outside my window.
That it is blue. That it is blue phosphorus
runoff, blue algal blooms, blue-tumored

muskrats slick in blue chemical afterlife.
The terrors of skin between me, dried fungal
lips unable, unable. Locked in a room by myself

as a girl, I did it on purpose. I closed myself
into the woolly carpet, turned off the lights
and sat as a pilgrim over her vial of cyanide.

I slept with my body pressed to the door.
What defines the loss of will but this:
that I did not care for anyone to let me go.

LAND OF SWEET WATERS

But the husband is an idea that occupies and tills the idea
until you are outside of it. And I wanted for so long to sing
an unlonely ode, but the ode requires a centering, a centering
for which I am outside. Or I slept in the husband bed, or made
many men sing. But I come from land that meant sweet waters
and nothing of the land bears this shape. But I sipped flat vanilla
Coke medicinally and scraped the innards of a shredded warren
from the new wood floors. Or I dropped a rock on a smashed cat's head
because it whimpered, stuck living on Lincoln Boulevard. How is it
I come from Glück's marshland without any of its blue lore?
My body stank in its magenta stirrups, my body rattled inside
the toppling trailer home. What origins was I supposed to speak to?
My identity, it means longing, a surname slipping into ur. A stranger
told us Eilbert means olive and we were so hungry we believed him.

CONSULTATION

Grace is a word that stings.
Megan Fernandes

When asked if I've ever attempted or begun the process
resolved to end my life, the decades' past dandelions throw up

their heads. Radiant silence. A type of yellow. Her hair.
I could mouth off and hit them all with branches torn in a clearly

violent way, a likeness to hurricanes, a left-rattling subwoofer.
Decade of acid rain. Decade of smog. Of ozone holes and the green-

house effect's definition glaring from the new-edition earth science
textbook. When the stick was a brain that cracked against my head.

I tell the story of the highway. When I stood in front of it like a cartoon
facing real life. The no hands that grabbed me back. The headlights

that might not brake in time. From the top of the highway, on a clear day,
you could see the Manhattan skyline that we called *the city*. Blinking

needles. The Twin Towers like rat incisors. I ached to be launched there,
but only so I could touch it, pummel the silver line. Nobody was ever

around to guard me like a ghazal. I put a thumbprint to the white
beef fat congealed in the Folgers can. I pushed down into its sludge.

A story in reverse is still a story. It is the sting of hay grass stooped low
in the corral. It is AM radio crackling a gray man's voice. Hands cranking

the wheel left as headlights soaked my figure. The panicked cartwheel
of the service road opening into a Hess. Green-and-white candy above us.

Cold Butterfinger, a can of Coke, the expressway exhaling beneath us.
Her hair. Italian black. Radio silence. I held my chin up the whole time.

EDGE HABITAT

I have fisted a landful of grass and I have rubbed it. I have rubbed it
across the torso of my belonging. These little possessions, how I fiend
on them, call them mine. My pockets lined with cuts. A satin, leaking gel.

I do not miss the world I never asked for. That's not it. A house is nothing
but a suffocation of grasses. None, I want. I force a newborn from my mind.
A limb entwined with mine. I forget the word for *minefield*. I walk in this

forgetting. The swirl of my daughter's hair is silken, not there. I wade in
the muck of not, brothered by gray waters, fugitive dust. A new mother
on Instagram, the caption, "Babies smell so good." But I can't. The wind

cuts a line across a stone lion slowly. It takes years to etch. Programs
emerge, calls for new budgets, mitigation plans, new insurance laws.
Let me contain this how I cannot the girl I dreamed named Daisy. A

dehisced sprout. Poison ivy, its ecological importance. I dig into my tote
bag and produce a recording device. To record this interview, do I have
consent? Fat white berries fruit as birds migrate south. A new development

pumps up leaded water, an offering. The daughter blooms as a throat constriction.
I respond to dating apps. Something mothers in me as it did when I read
the suicided student's poems. Bees are the hive or the loss itself. Something erases

in the green. But the words are sometimes beautiful. Cadmium. I am not
phosphorus. Nor iridium. A world outside leaches in. I equivocate when
pleasured. I lock the door, bolt it shut. And I itch at the borders of subdivisions

in my head. Learn I am not no longer not immune to the urushiol of contracts,
the living oil of greedy men constructing high-rises and future evictions. Concrete
partitions to keep a fire burning one unit entire. The exurban dream of it all—

to enter is to have the ability to exit. My throat inflamed with understory, its
diminishment part of an incremental payment plan. You wished me to understand
top-down economics, third-party predators, the moneyed saliva of ownership.

Daisy in chains, a daughter I never. A housing agent screams into a bouquet of mics and far from here, the ivy tickles the snout of a doe. She disappears like a Cher song into ambient techno frost. I carry the elsewhere buzz of life under my nails, digging.

THE LAKE

I walk sure to my door with a key, my pulse, my
        fucking doggy bag. What is the wind, what is the blaring
mind that makes   each morning shatter into appearance,

        the men I have ripped from the IV drip, for whom thirst was once

thorax deep, a sharp asiago souring absolution

into memory, the ways I wake up forgetting. And how

        to live I must snap the ruler over my knee,
release narrative into the dust of future tense. Night a green mouth,

some future tyrant; thus a woman is born, the vowels
        blare out so only the words are left.

BACTERIUM

In the last segment, I tried sufficiency. They moved
my femur and a single woman braiding her hair fell

from me. I tried to warn you: this desert editorializes.
A scorpion lifts its tail, *braids* more active than *braiding,*

it hisses. I, of all people, get it. In the mornings we wake
to the kind of life we want until we turn our heads east.

The night fills without us but I warned you, I was full
already. A banana inside me blasted open a door,

my mind at the threshold of such a door blank. Love
transacts, a figure in the distance crowded with windows.

An enzyme eats plastic, but which kind? Synthetic polymer
or the ways you tried to keep me? This is the last segment.

My mother

draws a circle around time and this is an intercourse. My mentor
draws a circle around time and this is an intercourse. I shake

out of bed. Humans continue the first line of their suicide letter.
An enzyme invents us, we invent enzymes. The plastic we make,

we must eat it. Draw a circle around time. We designed us
in simple utterances. The political term *graft* means political

corruption. The grifter never had an *I*. In the burn unit, they
place tilapia skins over human wounds, the killed form on top

of afflicted form, also a graft. Also a graft of afflicted form,
the killed form on top, they place tilapia skins over human wounds.

In the burn unit, I never had a grifter, corruption
means political, *graft* the political term. In simple utterances

we designed us. Time draws a circle, we must eat it. We make
the plastic, enzymes invent *we, us* invents an enzyme to continue

the first line of a suicide letter. Out of bed I shake with intercourse.
Time draws a circle around my mentor. Time draws a circle around

my mother.

This is the last segment. The ways you tried to keep me? Synthetic
polymer, but which kind? An enzyme eats plastic, crowded window,

a figure in the distance transacts love. At the threshold of such
a blank door, my mind opens a door. A banana blasted inside me.

Already I was full but I warned you, the night fills without us.
We turn our heads until we want the kind of life in the mornings

we wake to. I get, of all people, it. It hisses. A scorpion, more active
than braiding, braids its tail, lifts the editorialized desert. You tried

to warn me from me. Her hair fell, braiding a single woman. My femur
was moved. They tried sufficiency in the last segment.

GUNMETAL GRAY

Man's best weapon, how
we describe the dying ocean.

EAT AND KEEP

As for loneliness, I tire of staring at my pleading face
in a screen. A standing man burns always at the blade

of my door. I have never cared for any one readership.
I was happy to pretend my life back. I coughed up skin

into my palm, and here before me was my worth. The
standing man smells the vomit in my hair and tsks.

I miss the touch of the standing man. As for memory,
a cat blinks smashed in the road as I leave it. I thought

all horizons depicted mountains, and Dad could blast me
there from the hill my home stood on. That the rocks

would be brown and the purple fog a slip of cocaine
in the throat. Sorrow is not a deer stepping over snow

into its future, nor the idling car with a mother gassed
inside. It moves like the wet cloth of a mask flattening

the nose. The pixels show me troubled lights, but what
else? A buzz inside me pushes inside to out. How easy

I can leave me to it. I circle the day on a calendar and
reset my record. Birds scream in the past, a stranger at my cheek.

BONE

She keeps dreaming of the mother bear. A lumbering mass
that stalks her same path. Every morning, a graveyard preempts

her tasks. A memorial. A cemetery on her way to the errand.
A new ghost bike dressed in gaudy white. She would like to

stoop smally in a field. Tufts of hair loose in her hand. She
dreams of mother bear but is thinking how she ruined him again.

The blond baron crowded with sticks and mud, a golem or an Adam
or a history of inferior men. She desires only the smallest parts:

the mother bear licking her paw, claws asleep to the day. The girl
goes to no field, follows no other path. She scrolls her phone and sees

the feed as a future memorial. Something fleeting and uncaught,
a lake drowned in black screen. O, the hot takes and discourse,

a waking in never-elsewhere. An infinity of sameness. What hell
to have a center. Something for threads and core work and blood.

The mother bear who survives a shot to her heart. The skin blessing
the bullet around the bullet. In her kitchen, the kitten shit clumped

in perfect clay. The man told her he could easily kill her with the crook
of his arm and she thinks of her grandmother in love with a man

who reddened her daily. The journal she kept where she wrote *If I took
the crook of your arm, would I be a thief?* and the mother bear returns

to obscurity, and she breathes in the black lake, and she breathes in the black lake.

IF EACH DAY I LOSE MOMENTUM

If each day I lose momentum. If I thumb
through poems awaiting god's heat. If I

was not made in the image of god's heat.
In a boat in Cancún, I believe, the sun

sunk below, that is where I moaned
out one body, moaned into another.

If each day I lose momentum. If I can't
help that I'm a loud lover. If a window

opened long ago and I never dusted
off my knees. Any minute could have

killed me. His car plowing over the yard.
The possum he hit with intent. Indelible.

Hand to hot skillet, I pray my neck
won't break, but to whom do I pray?

If anosmic, I cannot smell a thing today
but red onions in a bag. If each day wakes

me up and I wake outside it, then I'm done.
Then I'm bored. Aren't you? Things I've never

had: a husband and child's nails to cut.
A cab driver asks about my son or daughter.

When I say they don't exist, he asks, *Why
not?* The moans that made me I do not make.

If I writhe lifeless on a bed with dignity, wet
sheets beneath my squirms. If I've never prayed

beyond a body gripping me. Our motions
slick, serene, empty. Love is a donkey's bent ear,

its haunches so much more useful. If I am
still capable. If I sing at the ceiling. Is this

all I'm to have? I remain abstract, washed,
a body brimming habit, in thrall to image.

THE LAKE

I dream that I reach across the bed

and kiss you with certifiable heat. Warm, clean heat. You kiss

back, the perfect swell of tongues

to melt away agendas, one finger gorgeously crooked

inside, heat and no fear of the heat until

I remember this is not our way. Cold skin of yogurt,

probiotic bodies alone in our positions, no gel

to make of ourselves, no mealy viscous of what?, just

memory respecting nothing.

Never have I been in a weather

more like my moods. Torrential

downpours for only a few minutes followed by

sunshine and distant rupture. A rainbow

arching somewhere, senseless gift of light. I have no

right to it, only the lies that

snap a prism into metaphor. Lightning without

rain, like the smart of a slap without

a hand. Thunder rumbles for hours.

❖

I put on a dress,
empire waisted, the rest of me moves and sways
inside garment's husk.

At last night's reading
a woman read a nice poem about a
barbecue involving her pregnant sister,
and after she read her nice poem

she said when she writes she never
expects her family to read it

and so with this nice poem her sister
did read it and lovingly pointed out

perhaps it went another way.
Laughs.
It was a nice poem about a barbecue
and I almost ran
from the room remembering when

my parents were confronted by my aunt's boyfriend
who said my life was tragic, didn't they think

it was tragic and they blinked

and they read it, they read me and we will never

talk about my tragic life.

It is like the back of my thighs,
no matter the extent to which I jog
and squat and downward dog, there is
a look to my thighs like the ridge of a
dragon's mouth, rough brush of skin I can't see
to hate enough.

But that it is there

         like Oppen's sublime image of deer chewing

alienly in a field

    that it is there at all

life's tragedies

      life's little, little tragedies.

Have I forgotten how to live?

        I dream of cancer not

as a disease but as many sheets wrapping

           the body until the body

disappears. The warm wrinkle of brutality.

      Rebecca Solnit writes of the violence

of climate change, that to "revolt

        against brutality" we must

"revolt against the language

      that hides that brutality."

    I read this before sleep and panic

      for hours, not asleep,

the world I hide in myself, the selfish will

    of information, the blood replaced by nitrogen—

what is blood inside the body   but a metaphor for hidden brutalities,

    the crowd of red crowned by skin, throne

thrown into phonic droves.

      Music thirsts for narrative, leeches

narrative of story. And so where do we stand

        on the artist's statement when

the poem is a vampire
in want of no further information—

the heart's clotted data
I find difficult to name.

What is the locus
of the project, the tea not steeped,
eucalyptus shine of earthlings—

I would like a poem to be postcountry

having decided that the most
significant change
humanity can make
is a complete flushing out
of borders. My body hangs
desiccated as an epic, a bell jar
busily showcasing. I vacillate

urgencies, the lyric rush I am so good at,

a pink that honeys the cheeks
with total isolation,
panic a cud to be chewed in its crisis pasture.

How did I become of two minds—

the winds charm me

into a hardness I've never welcomed,
the letting in of seasonal influences.

The beauty of the isthmus is the
choice to stay isolated.

Dickinson describes the volcano
                as a confided secret of pinks,

my mind mid-crag mid-deduction—
           I am terribly, terribly alone.

The presidential debate is tonight
           and I am busy telling my students

to give their poems more specificity,
                then less specificity.

Hypocrite Me who balances a lifetime
        of shame on the unsaid,

who relies on Stevens while shunning
           white supremacists, Stevens

      who, I understand mid-read, wrote in order
to know anything, to create

        a new topography based
on imaginative inquiry.

And so the racism, the sexism,
      what was that, what does one

make of the behavior of poets?
                 Not much.

The debate is tonight, the first of many.
I don't know what to say.

        Am I experiencing nightly panic
attacks or is it the multivitamins

     kicking in or is it my lack
of nutritional sense and these daily runs.

I get home. I'm to take a deep breath in,
    but hell how have I gone

this long
    breathing out—

IMAGINAL DISCS

*Repeated trauma in adult life erodes the
structure of the personality already formed,
but repeated trauma in childhood forms and
deforms the personality. The child trapped
in an abusive environment is faced with
formidable tasks of adaptation. She must find
a way to preserve a sense of trust in people
who are untrustworthy, safety in a situation
that is unsafe, control in a situation that is
terrifyingly unpredictable, power in a situation
of helplessness. Unable to care for or protect
herself, she must compensate for the failures
of adult care and protection with the only
means at her disposal, an immature system of
psychological defenses.*

Judith Herman, *Trauma and Recovery*

One survives the desire of another. Another aspect forms.
The brother trolls. The brother fathers. The brother still-

born. Still I saw the teenager every day, his twisted gait. My
friend didn't speak to me for a year, mad I disappeared to

play with _____. I am surrounded by brothers. A filament
glows like a match absorbing flame, it glows well past its

ending. One has grown tired of repetition. One is in
awe of long-term romance. The year I threw myself out

of the bedroom, images of my family piled up in a corner.
The year of Zoloft. Someone else's bedroom I stunk up, I

yellowed the foam. I am surrounded by hotlines. Call back
in the morning. It always went that my dad drove an errand

with a gun to his head. In the film he'd be credited Hostage
because one would be all it would take to send a message.

The year my nose bled from panic. The brother edits his
comment. My mom opened the door, home at the wrong

time. The year my hair fell out the side of my head. When
will I bore of repetition. The year I loved so hard the decade

pressed me into a pillow. So many teenage boys. The hard-ons
of stoners bishoped in the night to me. The hymen cooled

in the snow. The hymen dry as my wits in the classic night
I was driven away. The teenage boy sits me down to lecture,

presses himself in. The year of out of order. When will repetition
bore through me. Why. They needed to die in a narrative way.

CRESCENT MOONS

When the forensic nurse inspected me, she couldn't
see the tenderness he showed me after. My walk home

squirmed sore with night. I passed the earthworms
displaced to sidewalk, their bodies apostrophed

in the sun. I did not anticipate a grief
so small, my noun of a prayer, *Eat dirt to make dirt.*

Took a man's hand as he led me to cave. So long
as I breathed, I could huff violets in his dank, practice

earth's gasp. Mother lifts daughter, daughter casts
look at camera, a killer, a stick in the mud. I hold

my own hand. When the forensic nurse inspected
me, I described the house, historic blue. Asked me

to push my hips down. Little crescent moons
where his nails stabbed into me. She gave me

the word *abrasion* so gently I offered consent. Blue
as the moon when I sighed *wait,* blue as the *no* of my

throat. *Abrasion,* possibly extended form of *red.*
Harm must always preempt a starry night, many galaxies

scraped under the nail of a heavenly body. Ah, my
second earth, its wounds hardened into swallowed

prophylaxis, an injection pooling between muscle
and skin. A waking seed. Dead-armed antimoons

aggregated. A storm can loft seeds up to thirty miles
away. They dust the sidewalks like lost data.

He did not intend. *Did not.* Bloody speculum
a telescope searching the angry night sky for proof.

THE RITUAL

When my brother died I wasn't yet a body. When I entered,
    the orderlies wrapped me in the traditional red velvet frills,
a woman said my name until I could say my name. We called each other
    Mother until I learned she was Mom and I was Natali-a, Natali-a.
In the moments when I woke up, my brother shifted to become my
    walls. I slept in his bed. I stepped on his shaggy brown carpet. I drew
a heart directly onto the dresser to mark his place. The photographer
    lined us in a row like Coke cans. My two living brothers pressed around me,
a shark toy in the gap of my teeth. The photographer propositioned
    my father in the next room. My gums fondled the plasticine, a thrill
to feel with a surface beneath my teeth. The chorus teacher came
    and fed us lyrics to a song we would sing. We would sing it
lit against the great tree hanging his name and other names for death,
    Daniel a bauble, his body a bauble, his life a bauble I wanted
to jam between my teeth. A guitarist played Eric Clapton, the song he
    wrote for the dead son who fell from a window while Clapton's head
blackened with heroin. The woman I called Mother strung gold with her
    twelve-string, her son still dead. I took clay into my cheeks to make
my brother live. I thought this was how things went. A machine takes away
    a brother and replaces the brother with a Knights of Columbus,
Styrofoam coffee, cheddar wedges, crudités, Budweiser and Chateau Diana.
    I have dreamed of every gone friend this year whom I did not place
on baubles and who I don't suppose is dead.
    My brother slithers up in his larval sac in love with the fear
that embalmed me to his absence. The photographer shows me the famous
    photo of my siblings, and before he can die, I jam the image
through every plastic row of my teeth. A part of me is full of joy.

MALIGNANT

With any luck, I will be beside a tree
        when he finds me. I will have whittled my sense
of determinism into a ginger, called its shape mandrake,
        and let my voice milken against the stillness
of some other life. When will memory be usable, no, not
        useful, as in having the potential of action, as in
when I left my house behind and let him drive me,
        what was the house anymore but a distillation, a tree's
jutting roots without trunk or limb. I mean not to call the
        home an association of life and wood. I mean
I am working on a novel and cannot exit interior monologue,
        no matter what I do. In this sense the memory is
usable, the effect of eight billion streaming scenes weaponized
        for once, for once. The days I've always diluted through
sieves of comfort, explanation a way to talk about winter.
        Or it was that to speak was to winterize the body, the year
I did not speak and the unspeakable girded me to the
        repulsion of self. The novel, S reminds, is an idea of reality
as well as the reality itself, modernity a life form
        old as Cervantes, the casual gaze tearing open the animal.
The man walks like a theory of man toward me. When
        he arrives, I will open my throat to show him how I've lived.

Or it was that to analyze the novel, I had to return to antithesis,
        a bludgeoning of sound without a creature to produce it. Last
night, I read Ferrante. The window open. Night rehearsing
        through that window. Across the street, the Lutheran church—
I who have never entered a church without the creaturely
sensation of heathen, I the glamour of damned profligate
        Jew. Across the street, a retching sound, from man or
the approximation of man, for its retch like none, a
        machine scraping a tree's side, a sidelong wound

shaped in the grease of life or terror. Narrative economy,
that is, when one chooses to ignore simultaneity or coincidence

      if it troubles delivery; I could not bring myself to the
window, I could not accept the trouble of simultaneous life.

      And even in mindfulness, the overlapping reels that affect
modern retellings, the body distressed and in need of help,

      the way I was so recently distressed, a fuse line dudded
before ever knowing the verb of its source, I

      shut the window, I closed the blinds. The church's driveway
held the splash of vomit, but it would always deny the man.

      I lit incense, cued up a baking show. The absence
of the question where I sit round and warm in idiotic answer.

Or it is my body that is the question, looping and tearing

      as in the interview exchange today where I told *Salon*
"There's a terrible irony in wanting more from a lessening," when

      asked if I ever lost weight for a performance. Of course I have.
I'm a woman, I'm doing it right now. Have trouble with the lyric, see its guise
as the gesture of the lyric not at all, the empty room I work hard to

      furnish. But then the novel, why *novel,* word like a cascade
of black ants, a blood order, a crushable assemblage on the stoop,
many crows heavying a wire, lifting in a dead way toward,

      toward what? And here we are, a cinema amid death,
an image to bind us in the ravaging. The novel as I see it, spitting,

      a prescription from Lispector, that is "something still being
torturously made." Let me call the scene an insurrection.
Let the crow light on the railing of the mansion
next to the Lutheran church, let it shit passively as it

      blinks in a scavenger's way as we all blink in a
scavenger's way. Let it spread and ruffle and cackle.

      How its verbs form a woman, what is left to take
from our bodies once we dry out, thighs a trembling attempt

      of the infinite. Of course. And how I am a tree, the mutability
      of every tree, the page of every poem.

Or I am thinking about the word *aboveground,* irrespective of nothing
　　　or it is something that moves me about being, to force up land
that it might be all around me, indemnifying me to a course, how every-
one worries over my bones when I can't move from bed, dreams swarm
　　　so that I might vector usefully in any given direction. After the fire
my mother's silence was the pool, containing the green water of October,
summer's forgetful heat that leads only to neglect. Then I discovered a poem
　　　written in year twenty-three, that the abuser tried to drown my brother
and I called this a footnote in my life. Always the pages of literature compel me
　　　to change, or at least to the effort of dramatic mobility, that flattening
way we each become a surface in order to be read, deciphered. Ferrante
　　　asks me to reconcile my thinnesses, the girlhood stretching far into
adult limbs, like a poisoned root that swells into a nameless tree, like how
to illustrate distance, one must modify the noun, that it isn't a novel I'm writing
　　　but a series of injunctions that matter only to earthen things, that
there is law for the rock only insofar as there is a rock at all. The rock garden
　　　bordering the pool, the noun that enables abovegroundness, how
when after the fire, many men surrounded me and collapsed the pool,
　　　green water returning to the grass, and isn't it beautiful, how
even as the chlorine failed to clear the water, it bleached the grass.
　　　The chemical spilling into what we never did name.

IT'S A GIRL!

In the first segment of the last landscape, you pick up
old poems you've written. They are the first poems you

considered worthwhile. Your mother leads you
to the master bedroom to show you your birth cards.

People now dead congratulating you on being born. They say
*Natalie Dawn—we hope you are a good girl—*and mud

floats up your throat, the filter of a cigarette trapped
in the waste bin, the note to Catherine telling her and

scribbling out just when he let you go from between his
legs. You remark on the roundness of your face. So sixteen

and precious. What a little baby. Three years earlier
he reached into your body and presented you the stone

of your name. Ah, Aunt Rose sends her love to the girl,
the members of the bereavement group say *rainbow*

rainbow. Daniel was the only boy for whom your parents
threw a baby shower and Great-Grandma didn't come

out of superstition. In his death, no more showers. A crib
from the money guarded the rest of us. A cage of blond

good luck. In the next segment, a letter you wrote and
a letter you crumbled. You tell us Daniel is the best boy

among us because he turned blue and stopped. You dream
and it is wretched as the horse whose hair was rinsed

with flame. You swallow spinach and it is wretched as
the origins of immolation, a sauce sprinkled with sacrifice.

The night is dense and you rest alone. You rest and it is
a boring sentence. You flare your cheeks. Dark seams of

skin taunt your body. A brother is dead who had never
lived. Isn't this the curse? Light not a trick but a necessary source.

DO NOT INTERVENE

The girl took the skull to the rim of a lake
and stared at her own skull glimmering back.
She rinsed the skull of matter and placed it

like a sailboat into the water, the water so still
we can call it the absence of a mind. She prayed
that the skull was the skull of a wolf but she isn't

a lucky girl, only the lucky girls find such mandible
fortune. In truth, the skull must have been a deer
felled in the gamma wave that obliterated kindness.

We are not what we ever were. The planet spit us
back, a seed in its mouth. Now we rinse the dead
by the rims of lakes. We trace the jaw for flesh, hairs,

anything that might indicate wind pushed through
fibers of life. The girl removes a tick from her arm,
the flabby biceps extra juicy for the Ixodidae who rule

these parts. With her nails, she pinches her flesh
first, sacrifices blood to explode the suckling parasite.
She dismembers the tick body from her fatty riches

but the head digs deeper, wants to swim in her forever.
She returns to the skull. She returns to rinsing it
as if the world had ever heard silence, as if sound

even existed without our need of it. In the grass, she
pushes four fingers inside the eye socket. She tries
to recall the hand that folded laundry. Soft fabric.

What she wanted with this collection of skulls
is what we all want: a moonlight capable of love,
a moonlight that shows us we can still live here.

PSALM FOR THE WORLD BELOW

Some day, perhaps, remembering even this
Will be a pleasure.
Virgil

In bed, I rub my legs
against the dirt I brought

into the sheets. The last
man who held me tendrils

thick with old ceremony.
A blight of granules

on my skin. What is it
I want? I should discuss

the sky, trauma's ocular,
or the basement crickets'

godless feathering. They darken
when I near. I held his

gaze until I couldn't.
Ascending stairs to earth,

I, a Dido, flawed to love
"a thing forever fitful."

As in the day a lily bloomed
on my Chinese evergreen,

white yonic elsewhere,
I showed him this gift.

It leeches energy, he taught me.
Cut it off. I lock-screened

my gift as it withered to spit.
Outside warms whatever clovers

mother the paucity of bees,
my landlord ass-up in the weeds.

When did master gardeners
take over my life? Wasn't

anything grown that didn't
need his pluck or his pluck?

Great men all stumble,
hands grasping wineglasses,

undone by figures to cheaply
desalinate oceans to irrigate

the Sahara and Amazon.
All directives require revenue,

a his-pluck to his-pluck to his-.
Pinot soaks the flannels of men

as they kiss my peached skin.
They measure air, they teach me

I won't change a thing.
The Fates hold no settlement

for us. What is it to change?
Home calls. A father speaks,

a mother listens. They occur
like a sink full of water, voices

a cloth submerged and unclean.
What is it to vow to that

which flaws us together, apart?
What is it to say *This is the man*

I love? I shimmy off a dress
in the equine rot of night.

My cheeks are still supple,
they assure me. Richter plays.

Listen, he taught me. If he
held me, I held him back.

THE LAKE

An attempt was made. I told S that we are not
the sum total of our mistakes. I said it
as I believe I am the sum total of my mistakes.
I consulted Lisa Robertson for guidance:
"The truth is, everything that isn't poetry bores me."
I think this must be true because some days
I state its opposite. Saturdays pour through my body
like tea water. I see the shape of my face
in the steam of a mirror. I do not want to see
the shape. I have been staying with S for a number
of reasons. I am scared. I want to place me
on a hook and back slowly away, and the theoretical
desire clings me harder to ego. Poetry bores me.
The weather bores me. I open my mouth to nobody.
I push my body against no body. The sky opens and I think
of Geryon's red wings, that in text he must stretch
in secret for us to see the small mutiny of cells. Cells
paned to cells, lonely like mythological scales.
I walk with a black tourmaline tucked in my bra,
and my lower back snaps when he calls me. He
was once the dominant *you* in this poem, but
is there any house so strong it couldn't burn? Where
lies the vocative in the symptom of elsewhere?

                              My arms
slack against me, they move toward nothing
but the weight of arms. The truth is I fumble
in a clever way and mean every word of it.
When I read the word *house,* I see a line of windows,
cells paned to cells, a train whistle. Is this what
insouciance feels like? I note on my phone
to write a poem called "The Door in the Corner,"
but the story of the Dogon door is not my story.
The relief in the Malian wood is not my relief.

I have protected myself as best I could. It did not
keep me safe.

Wake up on foam. As a teen attended foam
parties, hands groping with muted fire toward
                    not hands, a mud queen

wallowing to scrub limbs clean, a notion I lightly
stole from Virginia Woolf. I am nibbling
            a Gruyère croissant as if it were

my own stopped heart, a polite hunger to stay
breathing. I can extract necessary fats from my
loneliness, cheese hardened in its spill out of pastry,
an abstraction of its former surface: a prebirth burst
            frozen mid-ooze. I ingest the ghost

of degrees, sip coffee picked by scabbing
fingers. Eudora Welty says of *To the Lighthouse*
that when she opens the book she is "still unwarned,"
her awe, her delight "forever cloudless."
                    To be unmoored, as I am,

I consider the sublime.
A moor is different from its fastening, and I prefer
the proposed etymology of a *moor,* that it might share
            roots with *lake* and means *to die.*

A moor, in this sense, is a dead land.

Mi amor, my joy is I have filled pages with
my signature. I have only just noticed the first section
of *To the Lighthouse* is "The Window"—how
did I miss this, in all my years of reading: "It was when
she took her brush in hand that the whole thing

changed." I have only just noticed, then, the best
kind of windows are doors, doors
                    the worst kind of windows.

I am free from terror, you see, and only terror is free.

But Eudora Welty said *unwarned.* And I think of times

within books I too have been unwarned. *The Descent of Alette.*

Watership Down: "The primroses were over."

I spotted a recently dead rabbit ahead of me

on my run this morning. I had that sense

of death in the near distance, a pile of death, until

my brain replaced death with leaves and trash, until

my eye was over the corpse, saw its black eye freshly mute.

To witness death, the only trust on earth, to then be in

        its range, my throat

crowded with soft moons as a fig is a slaughter of seeds

shocked by their release, as if flesh contains only the stories

        of sutured lines.

A rabbit. A rabbit with its eye pointed skyward.

I remember when I learned of monocular vision;

the ability of an animal to see two sides thus spoke

      to its taxonomy as prey. And I thought

I thought of my optometrist father

      who said there was an invisible eye in the space

between our human eyes, so the world is rooted in our perfect facial symmetry

that we might see our damage, the curl of stopped masses—

and in the years since, all my charcoal

      portraits ruined in the middle,

one faint eye erased between the eyes

         and this my understanding then

of how we survive.

      A rabbit with its one eye pointed skyward,

it appeared as stone, black crystal

polished smooth to pacify the afternoon.

              And yet

the eyes will be the very first to go, vitreous humor

for the small machinery of life, death squad

        by any other name, maggots wriggling

      beautifully

with life. And yet, the shock of its body, inexplicably limp.

I thought of nothing but the word *fresh*.

    It was freshly part of death, a homecoming

parting the leaves

        to behold a browning parade.

The space of life and death

    ruptured by amateur sketch marks.

To experience wind of this strength

    I feel singular, planetary weight on my skin.
I brace for the weather like a lusty man,
        a column rising between my eyes. More debates

have been planned. A bee lands on my fingertip
in a pleading for stillness and I call off the war,

    allow it purchase.

The word *still* becomes itself like all words do.

Except there's this wind, associated with
        the color blue, associated

for the sky alone, the way loneliness clings to grammar
only as we need it to reach others.

        I suppose I am happy

to perform gone. My father texts me

Gorgeous in response to pink leaves.

There is nothing, I mean,

about the color pink that doesn't feel hurt.

I'm gone in the bracing weather. I'm gone in the
bracing weather.

At last night's debate, I had to leave the room.
I had to e-mail my therapist, say simply
I don't feel good.

And isn't it a privilege to dump my suicide
on others and not die, for S to see

my hands blue and shaking, terrific with life.
I don't believe presidential candidates belong
in this poem,

they must be kept nameless apparitions

polluting the air with their visions.

It is quite how I see my attempts, an invisible

voice slumped atop a failure inventory.

I distrust the power of powerful names
and yet I tell my students to write
with intentional ambiguity
and gall forged with precision.

Woolf, early in *To the Lighthouse,*
writes about the prose of salt, on boredom perhaps,

and I think of the prose of salt,
the bored light I have missed slumped

              atop a failure inventory, panic
igniting the roan hills of my heart

        with metal. My breath rank
with bile and caffeine, such is my comportment,

a tongue bright with fool's gold
        a crisis inarticulate slick,
        a crisis forged with precision.

CHIPPEWA FALLS

Breaking news leads tend to rely on a passive voice. Someone
was found dead. A legislator was convicted. The story isn't about

the man on a walk with his child when they come across the body
of a little girl on a walking trail. Their role, tucked into a verb that

also means *be*. April 25 will be a day marked by a billionaire
buying something that rots our ego minds; it will always mean

more than a murdered girl. I sever an onion and think of the man
who left us a voicemail calling us cocksucking communists

for writing about race in local politics. Ire a ring of onion skins
caught on the ear, a girl murdered, and reason, that dumber poetry

that presents a bleached bone instead of an orchid. There were
the men who shoved women in front of subway trains in the '90s,

and I'd stand on platforms holding my body like a stanza.
All the girls and women tripped and mocked and groped,

writhing under skin, knitting organs into bricks. There was
a girl who liked the color purple. Thaw gushed the river.

A ten-year-old was found dead today.

VIRGIN PSALM

My childhood nosebleeds challenged
the question of blood capacity, drops
at first like a kitten's soft menstruating
in the snow. Wet warmth spread
across my upper lip, the pleasure I took in
horror. You can't know the relief when
in the years that followed my hymen
broke and I wiped myself clean in the snow.
I thought it meant safety for the girl who lay
supine three years prior, the blood like time
a flag to wave the body's involuntary permissions.
I would die for language as language dies in blood,
a loss, a loss, a loss. C who said to me
you're a virgin until you bleed, and who was I
to question such human law. Do you get it?
This is what we do: become auxiliary enough
to be removed. *Blood on the Pontiac* rings true
like my love for the word *buckskin,* a word
shaped in my mind like a palindrome without
the promise of form. Last night I could not sleep.
I dreamed in shallow passage about the ex who
on his knees begged in the dark to strip and take me.
And it felt like supplication, the saint's wantless work,
to heed the man toward heaven, toward heaven.

THREE OF SWORDS

In my phone is a   phrase that indicates logging,
recording, taking down.   Terms that,
outside of phones,   imply other violences.
In my phone, I wrote   without context,
"In the Great Pain   of Missing You,"
notable for   what I can't say to him.
I am not worldly   enough to know
a river cuts through   country to return
to its coarser self.   I couldn't know a sea bleeds
fresh through the cut   of country.
What was the point of not   having a belief?
To lean left toward   no deity and pray for the
ruins as god places my palm   over a river. And since
god is the four-letter word   I can't pronounce,
I press my thumb over   the Home button to view
an image of rivers.   I cannot tell my father
I love him because   I have aged enough
for him to press   his thumb to my crow's-feet
in agonized appraisal.   I stand alone in my love.
Outside, a bunny   chews in black. Something alien
tears through nocturnal   life: the shrieks irrelevant
in sleep, a death so small   it cannot complete.
A planet cleaves itself   into another as a gosling,
hatched too late, coils   in mucked frost, abandoned.
In myths, the babies spared   represent miracles;
otherwise we would need   to name the dead blue-coiled
fists quotidian, blank.   My brother Daniel, gone
in the flush of myth's miracles.   In the Great Pain of Missing You,
things are going really well.   The fish float, from which
we get the phrase *belly up*.   They gleam phosphorus runoff
as fishing lines tangle   around the necks of turtles. A death
so small it cannot complete.   My mother howls
in chronic pain many states away   as I pull up
my comforter to sleep. Outside,   a dog whimpers

for an hour, concludes.   When I'm asked about my family,
I look out the window. How long   must I wait
to be missed by anyone. The snow salts   idled headlights.
Images of my naked body fill a screen,   arched ribs
and hips, a purling wet. There was never terror we couldn't see.

WET SEASON

An Orbit gum pack on the sidewalk, I don't know how empty.
Just sitting there like a manuscript draft. Whole generations
of poetry devoted to the pasture have ended in die-offs. I look up types of

root death and learn only of a television show where someone
named Root dies. So what if in all the day the most eidetic image
flashes near a cigarette butt? In the time it has taken me to live,

tree cover has grown more rapidly than humans could cut them
down, and it grows mostly elsewhere: former tundras, barren lands,
and mountains. Researchers call it a reflection of a human-

dominated Earth system. Understand this is not resilience
but upending crisis. I lick salty fat out of the bottom of a bowl,
do twenty squats and sit down for longer. Never will I be so brilliant

as the Orbit gum pack, the swish and green dazzle of plastic and
plastic and pulp. As the weather warms, the paper mills fill the air
with the stench of damp reams, a smell I'm told is money.

I hold my waist. I hold any part of myself that registers that spring
is coming. Hail in April as the floodplains widen, the soft presence
of FEMA ever at the ready where they never had to be.

Sometimes it's the word *turning* on the page that makes me buckle,
not the act, not the gesture. I see the light-year ago when I raced to Dad
standing at the door, always the surprise of arms, his jacket's chemical smell.

FIELDWORK

A sea otter carcass twisted on a beach. We scan
the beach looking for artifacts, find only bones.
The body gyrates after death into a pickled rag.
Along the forest road, stones move under our tires.
I learn of manuports, moving items
from one landscape into one they can't belong to.
In Alaska, I followed a falling feather of an eagle
and held it up to the sky, a gift. I carried it to New York,
a smuggled thing I couldn't understand at twelve. Body
cam footage released of the slain child. The eagle feather
kept for hundreds of thousands of miles and the gun
thrown behind a fence in fear. T asks if anything can be
an artifact. I think of handguns and horizon lines in the dirt.
Two hundred years' worth of buried surfaces. The archaeologist
raises a juvenile whale's dorsal fin she finds at low tide.
Artifacts must be altered by man, she tells us. The sea otter
on the beach died from its injuries. Broken backed and ravaged
by an orca pod. Eventually it will have never been here.
I track sand into the car, little grains of after on repeat.

WHITE NOISE

The ribbit of frogs or the buzz of a lamppost or the whoosh of a dishwasher

or the shriek of a woman at closing time or the rush of Durangos or the gull

cawing open the night. See, I am lonely for a touch that closed long ago, light

the way peach fibers are light, guarding the dumb heaviness beneath. The men

outside my window grumble, a confluence of drunks, the opioids funneling

their systems like rancid feathers in still water. So much of sense requires the

stupidity of memory, my head sliding down a line of crushed powder, chunks

of Percocet clogged in my sinuses. I can see it, the animal eyes of pain, a lowing

orange balled in their spines. The land upon which we bestow such grievances

never belonged to us and yet ownership is a funny drug, how it makes arms

reach for a wrong belief. Far below us, a jagged fault line, subduction held

together by the strength of friction. In the epochs the earth stays tense, we get

stability and the wealth of its wetlands. Far above the jagged fault lines, the

splash of beer vomit, mostly foam. To become myself, I stoop down and plunge

my tongue into a tarry mouth and gag until I have no name for any occasion.

I want to push my heart into a lightbulb. I want to see its light, smell its burn.

COUGAR KILL

My notebook slipped from my pocket as I grasped
hawthorns and Scotch broom for purchase. My last note

described the elk bones, the scattered tufts of hair.
How quickly a member of earth expires and sinks

into dirt. Slick furs flatten over bloating organs
as horseflies buzz and gorge. I know such hedonism.

When I scramble through thicket brush, I am not
thinking of pleasure, not the glorious bends of my back.

Skeletal remains appear always to lurch forward, a body
fleeing itself. The blackened flesh clinging to skull

shows no metaphor, because a metaphor should want.
Ahead of the body, we crush a path in search of the puma.

We look for a bed, find only where he dragged the cow
over a log. All skulls eventually smile in repose. I tsk at

a leaf-flat water bottle, a plastic doll with a caved-in face.
Somewhere, my notes tell a story in data. Seven molars.

Gnawed whistler tooth. GIS points. A spiral notebook
splitting and sogging in dense understory. I pull thorns

one after the other from my neck. I've disturbed ever,
everything I've touched. How dare I miss one thing.

THEY DO NOT EAT UNTIL THEY CLEANSE THEMSELVES

The triumph of the wicked is short, but the poor
rot in their earnings. Scarves wrapped to protect
against malignant atmosphere, a blue silk I took
from my grandmother's chest, nose pressed to its

mildews. It is prophesied that I will live through
one imprecise future. The couch holds me like an
indifferent mother and I didn't want to say this.
Because I can never get past the first holy book

I imagine the Gospels as good storytelling men
who pierce me with tender precision. There is no
agony in John, no garden in Mark. Synoptic, as in
we live each day with awful care. Scarves wrapped

to protect against malignant men, a yellow polyester
discarded on a bench, pink spray paint striping an
Aquafina bottle. The triumph is short but long, as in
a human life coiled in repose. My brother coughs

bloody phlegm in the grass, in need of its smell,
and I didn't want to say this. Because self-abandonment
is a novel being written, the drip that detaches my
uncle from his metastasis, and it feels wrong here

to confess the swift suicide drilled into my dreams.
No garden in Mark so I text a Mark with a garden,
a signal of my loneliness. I lie alone unable to stand
and I think of the John who crept his hand under my

shirt and the John who feigned sleep, his head sniffing my lap.
Every Matthew and Luke posed before comatose
cheetahs. My stomach stews with pinot, an apology of grief.
I touch my face and respire. I touch my face and respire.

FOR SETH

It's you who clear the thicket ahead first, your lank
body bending and straddling lines and edges of woods,
until it opens, as we think it does, to a sparkling blue bay

over which limestone cliffs cut. I touch the rock and hope
the energy travels the latitudes of the escarpment, New York
in another place, how odd that this is so. But I squash, for a

time, the insect inside me that needles in my ear comparisons
between here and home. I thought nothing would touch me.
Not the woodchuck sauntering along interstate grass. Not the

great white trillium flirting with a ruining earth. Not the lake
after which I named a book-length poem while wanting to die.
But there you are, stooping into a shallow cave to describe

Silurian rocks and agricultural runoff. The air smells wet, like

matter cursed to exist beyond all futures. We don't walk far
before we're kissing again, our breaths gaining heat, hands
feeling for our most ridiculous parts, which, I regret to say,

throb. My cheeks hurt from smiling in a nourishing way.
There's no fear of time, what it has done and what it will do.
With you I trust the day will open, as we think it does, again.

EARTH (THE)

On stolen land, I weep and refuse toast. I am told descriptions

of weather do not belong in the news unless the news is about

weather. Journalists should not describe the sky when reporting

on shootings. Chiaroscuro empowers the viewer to consider only

the focal point. I lick my finger to finger bread crumbs. I wash

my hands regularly. The virus "is not detected," according to my

lab results, a grammar that pacifies the lab findings and the host

into inconclusive entities. On stolen land, my heart aches for a man.

I read the latest local coverage. Implosions from a recent plant demolition

lead to respiratory infection and virus susceptibility in the thousands.

No one was told of the plan. Years ago an acquaintance said that

love happens all the time. *I think* and *I believe* are semantically

separate. We insist reason lives outside of faith. I think it will rain,

and I believe it will rain. To look at the sky. What it takes to look up.

THE LAKE

Ocean oxygen has been declining since before I was born—
I was born with eyes open to brine—A first photo snapped
as I crowned—Is it any wonder I crave how others see me
when I'm turned away—For reasons unbeknownst, I was
made from oxygen deprived of my older brother who died
before he had a chance to die—In infancy my eyes rolled
to the back of my head and I convulsed, suffocating—Doctors
believed my coma would render me damaged—I woke up—
Crowded by oxygen, the world keeps us—For now it spins
the way a story with no way out might—Lopsided arcs I
wake up within—Years ago a nurse predicted that I would
faint because circles crowded my eyes—Hypoxia,
an example of presence as absence, my body as the cooling
wake of my body—At bus stops, poisons travel with ease
through my blood—A man also poisoned tells me I'm sexy,
do I know how beautiful I am—In years my face will interpolate
new grammar as scientists calculate what is missing in the
missing—There isn't much to know—I stare for seven hours
straight at my new nephew—His name, like the ocean, is
Gray—Born alive—How easy language pretends utility, that
we become the isolation of meaning, meaning we are not—
How could we—Junk is all around us, scattering without
the confidence of metaphor—I stare for seven hours straight
at my newborn nephew—We grow beyond a road, always,
a neural pathway or a concrete, and it is no different, how we
come to loss, not when the ocean comas far away, the sea
a trembling memory of land—I do not mean to sound precious—
But what separates water and sea is economic function over
thirst—Theoretical newborns warm the future—Plastic elephants
and whales, creatures drawn into circles, black, happy eyes—
It is easy to see a single animal stitched into linen—There is
joy in misrepresentation—A polar bear swims impossible miles
stitched into its end—When a great land mammal sinks from
land, it isn't the past we care about—It is never present—I was

born with eyes open—The biomedical tools that delivered me
in 1986 fill an inch of underwater landfill—Everything made
gets discarded—Thermometers rust, a teddy bear molds, think gardens,
think—My nephew's eyes are gray—Each time he blinks, they darken—

My end isn't true yet—I am perhaps between distances—My
brother has updated his belief on abortion—I do not fight him,
I hold this white kin—My grandparents lived so we could be
praise of lineage incarnate—Headlines have accepted post-
extinction as a suitable mode—The sea grass persists in spite of—
Discussions of what the Great Dying looked like over millennia—
One can edit genes, the patent won—What makes women good
dancers?—Watch the hips—I am writing a novel about distraction
in the Anthropocene—It is necessary, our casting the
world aside to focus on the self as firm and business—What is an
image versus what is an expression—Which is the door and which
is the door having already slammed shut—In a dream my sex is
sewn together with thread made from a type of crystal meant to calm—
In my waking, the gynecologist pushes down and asks if I feel pressure—
I do—What might have strained these muscles, how long have you
experienced pain—The window or the glass that continuously melts
downward—In the last passage I meant to discuss the Wisconsin stars
so crisp in winter they cut the cornea—The heat that cooks the pavement
gum or the unseasonable sun—I say yes to dinner I say yes to drinks—
It isn't a choice that I live, not a conscious one—I explain to a man
that we have confused the direction of future innovation, that it never
amounted to high-rises or hovering cars—Instead we moved, but toward
the social—We have the equivalent of a hovering car in our hand, I
explain—I am sexy when I say this—I ooze a sexuality that bends our
normal equator line—Everything is bleached—Calamity as we see it
occurs without us watching—It does not give us the dignity—Marine
life fails without an audience—It will be the disappearance of marine life
that will conclude life on this planet—We have confused the direction of
catastrophe—We fail the water—The technology of everyday selfhood

does not capture the gradual collapse—Illustration of nautilus with
Shastasaurus or the pathogen-fighting sea grass they fear already gone—

See, if I am thirsty I can get up and walk to the spigot—A man
pardons the expression before uttering a slur—My eggs
poached perfect in the hungover air—I let a video run on under-
appreciated marine organisms and am shocked by the crunch
of a fish biting into corral—NoDAPL until the memes end—
What have you even done but sneer—Over the sea-dark wine
I imagine your voice cracking when it is done—When what is
done has not yet begun—Isn't that always the case—It is like the voice,
the speaker of a poem, when they figure out the device midsentence—
The valence shifts—Earthen only in how it is stripped—I
meant to tell you I have left but the sun was always shining—
The way everyone looks gorgeous when they say *sparkle*—Three weeks
ago an environmental activist died and I vowed I would not make
new trash—One napkin—One toothpick—Discarded red onions—
Not to mention that soap required to clean the dishes I ordered
to stay—The dishes, the knives, the spoon, the fork, the cup, the
table, how can this not become trash too when even terra-cotta
bottles of year four hundred (before the Common Era) become junk—
See, the future makes us prehistoric too, when words are talismanic
and removed from function—How to explain this yet—I was born—
To be born is the single most painful event of life, we shift in our
skull—One might say the pain ignites us into being, in the same
way boredom makes consciousness an indistinguishable bruise—
My nephew receives a cake decorated with gold curlicue letters
to say *best day ever* and the newborn receives it and he receives more—

When I said I was moving to Wisconsin, everyone
gave me a mouthful about winters—Just you wait,
they'd warn, excited—Language is an impostor of
history—Within history logging and rice cultivation

denuded Cambodian lowlands and no future remains,
according to the *Times*—I sit on a bench by thawing
Mendota in February—I too am part of denuding—
Soon the lowlands will be gone—*Denuded,* stripped away,
a word seen only one way just as flesh faces forward
to other flesh, inward still to the mess of us—We are alone
this way—I am alone most when I grieve through
language, when I become the privilege of language—
The sun against blue as a woman exclaims to her dog
how nice, how nice it is outside—Denuded as the boy
who runs on the solid part of the pond with his family—
Denuded as I sip my coffee from an undisclosed village
with undisclosed labor laws, as I sit in Lululemon and
Saucony and UNIQLO, the brands a denuding
industry—Denuding the species to find its economic
use—There was a laminated memorial in the mouth
of the Yahara for a woman who threw herself in
the summer I arrived, but it has disappeared—
And the gone do not care if they are missing—On the phone,
a man denuded of love tells me in gasps, *I want to spend
my life with you*—I feed myself a croissant and look up—
The family on the ice is no longer there—I search for a
hole—In need of forgetting—

We come back to each other bruised by the difference
in weather—I didn't know our love would survive, but
I believe in work the way I do not believe in the future,
work as in livelihood, what will remain—I jogged through hot
pockets of air in February—Heat like the new breath of
my nephew—This is to say, failure is not the fault of air—
Atmosphere responds like flesh does to a torch—On a
bad site as a teen I watched a pig strapped to a gurney
tremendously alive get torched by a German in white coat—
I do not remember why my fascination was what it was
about this site in general—A site that boasted snuff films

and goliath penetrations and Mister Hands—I think it's
that I was new, that I came into a life that was already
happening, that stole from me in such a way that trauma
was a video on loop, and so it made no difference whom
I spied in the midst of their torture—But the pig, it stuck,
its leg twitching with receipt of flame contact, not able
to run—And then I left the room wailing—My curiosity
a mistake—My father heard me screaming and came to me
and saw what I had done—In a way it was I who had burned
the pig, it was I who had made this torture viable, it
was I who led me into the room—And my father took a
look at the video and said of course they were German,
the Germans have no empathy, no sense of the Other—
I saw in that moment the Germans torching my Jewish
flesh and understood—It was Y2K and
Slobodan Milošević and another timeline of ethnic
cleansing—The heat in the air today was like history
as a sum total weight on skin—I do not have faith in any
of it, but I exercise anyway—I schedule dinners over Google
and hope for reconciliation—Did you know that ladybugs
secrete their own blood when they panic—Yellow streaks
I once thought were oil—What is blood but an issuing
of panic anyway—It is raining here and sunny on the pier—

Someone casually says *Earth is menopausal* and I trip
over myself this is so accurate—*Hot flashes* first attested
to in 1907—This same year in Russia, Ksudach
erupts—It is the last and largest recorded in Kamchatka, its own kind
of hot flash—In eighty years, I will be born—
In Anaheim a white cop shoots at Latino children and "no one
[is] wounded"—Two Latino children are arrested—White cop faces
no charges—The year is 2017—A grounding phrase to mark
time—My one-month-old nephew goes to the beach—His
sandy debut—I have already started this series but resist
telling my brother that I wrote his newborn into a poem about

depletion—One limning of menopause is "moon pause,"
another, change of life—I find a note in my phone,
I owe you money, followed by *The boyfriend of my*
girlfriend's best friend's sister—At the point of this writing,
C.D. Wright has been dead over a year—"Poetry is nothing if not
equipped for crisis," she assures from below—We watch in horror
from the terrace as two young men stand on the lake in seventy-
degree weather—I cannot call them morons because maybe
I am the one who cannot comprehend solid structures bound
by freezing and warmth simultaneously—What holds any structure
together but the word that names its shape—The apartment
I occupy does not have a kitchen table, for example, and so I pile
my dinner plate on top of a stack of books—How are books not
a table—It snowed three inches overnight after seventy-degree
weather for many days—Bolivia over time has burned millions of acres
of critical forest to grow soybeans to export as animal feed
in a commodities trade in America, for hamburgers, chicken, pork—
I do not feel equipped for crisis—In 2030, "there will be no forest left"—
What holds any structure together but the world that names its shape—
Is there a song you sing especially well—Have you considered this—

Rapid analysis of climate change requires people to discuss
weather patterns—Vigilance requires of us more than grieving,
but here I grieve—The other night I writhed in bed,
food poisoning was it?, the nausea mounting with a shattering
thunderstorm—A February downpour in Madison should be
unheard of, should be the sublime whir of snow—I retched over
a toilet, spilling everything but myself, the misinformation
of nightly weather, the sleeping body stuck to sheets, the night
the dreams the wind the body helplessly together—In the morning
ground covered in steam and snow, forty degrees colder—My
mind a fever, wrestling formulas into substrata, into law—
Recurring thought of a man breaking into my room—The expression
beating me senseless oddly liberates, suspends world order—
He stabs, bludgeons, when I try to run he jumps over the

stairwell railing, blade down, and drags me to the floor—I spring
to sit, do not ask for mercy—Ask what I have done in this life—
My cheeks still firm, sallow as the bile, despite—These are not
dreams but fantasies—In another thought a former partner
leaves marks when he slaps me so that someone notices and
there, in that moment, my behavior noted without language—
Today it is March third, I forgot to pay my lease on the first—
Pay it now—Throw my phone against the wall in white anger—
I have never had white anger—Blood striping my arm from raking
nails across in desperate sleep—I want to talk about today's
weather—Cold as it might be for the Eastern Seaboard, but not
the Midwest—I tell my therapist about these thoughts and she
reminds me of the violence that happened to me—Cosmic to hear it
drummed up in reference—Haven't I already become the actress
playing me, to be present and removed the way great pain thuds
within its warren—Not exactly a memory—The shadow behind it—
And in my dream this morning, I am woken by phone buzzing,
but a fruit fly had brought a segment of grapefruit to my face,
asked if I were its star and repeated *And the sun goes to die on the*
sun and the sun goes to die on the sun and the sun goes to die on the sun—

You're only revising the patriarchal order, not dismantling it,
I say to M about women breaking down other women—With M
in Chicago: a foldout bed and a stocky pit bull, unable to sleep
and so reading about the secret pandemic of US-approved chemicals—
Manganese and chlorpyrifos and tetrachloroethylene and toluene
and DDT and arsenic and polychlorinated biphenyls and mercury
and ethanol and lead and fluoride—I learn how the brain develops,
the chemicals that kill brain cells in development, the brain cells
that stop developing by the age of two—I do not sleep for sleep is like
the wind and trees amazed—I drank a seltzer before bed, the word
manganese gorgeous and tinny on my tongue—M and I talk about
recall failure this morning; B, in her sixties, says her trouble is
nouns, and I think, who is not troubled by nouns—We pretend
we do not use the earth by applying minimalism—Stark unnatural

white and bright cold steel—The problem is oxygen, too much
in mammals and too little in the ocean—The trace mineral needed for
living organisms becomes a neurotoxin when present in large
amounts—Yesterday the president rolled back stringent federal
regulations on vehicle pollution—Says too the pipelines must use
US steel—We are nothing if not a series of wrong chemicals—
We stare at fish at the aquarium and M asks about faces, specifically
why faces should be the thing significant—I don't know how to fill
spaces with anything but guilt—Isn't that a Jewish thing, I'm told,
Richard Spencer who used our language to say we are not people,
soulless golem, what is that—I tell M I'm in a confessional mood,
she says she is out-of-body—Sleepless I zoom in on X-rays
of heat spots on the in-utero brain, in control groups and in non—
Heat spots on the living ocean do smack of bad MRI results—
Magnetic resonance imaging, there it is again, permuting
doom—The language of the planet is a woman, why it is
we do not believe her even as she kills her own—

Last night I sat on a barstool and told a man
named Michael that my name was Michael—
I woke up as myself, with no better reason
to be myself—How easy it is for the lake to make
sound—The trees sing—I have not walked much
this morning, the day already broken in my throat—
See, my routine: Boil water, think of Chilean
suffering, humans suffering the impact of humans—
First so much fire that we cannot breathe, then so much
water that we cannot drink—See, my routine: Boil
water, stain water with grounds, let it build
a tar foam, plunge it down, make it a cup—Call it
Joe, as I am Michael—I can do nothing against
the Santiago death winds, sip from my yellow mug
on my yellow throw in my pretty pretty house—
Catastrophe a background color—When I wanted
to die, it was easy—I am doing it now—I crack

an egg into a bowl—Outside, an opossum heaped
in the kind of fate we expect for such creatures—
The yolk foul with old bristled fur—How it is
I still crave beauty in rot—I break the yolk
and pour it into the ritual—What I want to say:
Of the past, the car drives away mute as any
picture toward and far from what I know—
A man sits outside the frame and I understand
time to be speaking, wet texture filling with
mouth—I have no respect for what is said
of survival—I am thinking of the storm ahead,
peach bright, so goddamn beautiful I forget
there is a better idea in the future, the future
that promises only that it will never arrive—
It's what we want, isn't it, a rupture ahead
that has no name for what it will do—

The problem is that the daily record is artless—
I attempt constantly to start over—Monkey bread,
who'd have thunk it would taste that way—A movie about
two journalists breaking Watergate—Today is Easter,
the United States has killed over 250 Syrians in the month
of March alone, more than any other supposed terrorist group—
Exeunt with a dead march, the final cue in *King Lear,* why
the image always sticks—The issue is how facts eke through
sunlight—No way to avoid this—Artlessness as critique of the
way we must live minute after minute—The launch of war,
that we sit on the edge of the world, we must rely on love,
isn't that what one does—But it has never been like this before,
it is never quite like this—Why the daily record terrifies so
entirely, its unique hold on time minimizes public recording
somehow—Like right now I am listening to the new Future
Islands—I am thinking about a young buff Dustin Hoffman—
The world quakes and I don't know it over the speaker blasts—
How easy it is to be inside oneself without entering the body—

I've become conscious of my present condition, my
inability to manage a pretty image, maneuver technique into
a siren, the way the word *alarum* manages to be both pitch
and beauty stamp—Alarum, alizarin, an acrylic I loved only
in how I uttered it—I spread it on a canvas thick as a lie,
used it to make a dark sky darker—See, we need the archaism
of red, don't we—So here is an image—A wild turkey crossed
a busy road right in front of my car and I thought to get out,
gaze at the slow waddle, they really do waddle—What are we
to do with the animal that does not walk in the imminence
of death, that does not smell the copper dollar frenzied in
burning gas—Where is the mercy in geography—What do
you remember about the day—And did you drive around
the turkey too idiotic to be vulnerable—I have no idea
what a turkey smells like alive—I stayed in my car a long time—

Great Barrier Reef now 80 percent dead, now I declare
I want to quit the *I,* the verbs that keep I fed—The
budget cuts will end us, fragile federal research infra-
structure already buckling—Portraiture of death, limp
wrists pointing upward toward carbon-heavy winds—
It isn't clear when it will happen, but the next generation
sounds like a fantasy doesn't it, why I stare and stare
at my nephew, his gray eyes in the gunmetal future,
the paradox of firm, healthy glow—What does it mean—
I tell A that the word *and* has roots in both directions,
that it suggests a before (ante) as it also means next, that its
etymological record begins in the twelfth century—I
ask A what we did with things before *and,* how did we
navigate objects if we could not own up to a center—
Object of property—How did we see ourselves intermixed
with the elements if the combination of things could not
precede us—And I think about this because scientists
describe coral in the Great Barrier Reef as unique farmers,
polyps forming colonies and a limestone scaffolding on which

to live—The order of things relates directly to the kind
of home we are able to make—*Reef,* as from Old Norse,
to mean "rib"—Gnostic shadows in the fecundity of
absence—Human stain not yet its seepage but a theory
of influence—The rib ripped from the bosom of a man
and thrown into the sea as a godless ridge—Origin story
in which the reef contains the organisms that colonize
material to make the reef—The secret seems now that
the only story that survives is the story of the man
as he ends on the surface he refused to make—What we
did not do this time or any other is rely on our own rib
to thrive—Colors bleach, the planes imprint the white
scar, fried limestone, bone crooked in the sand, ruined
infant brain, the potential for growth yet one more
opportunity, a recapitulation of events forwarded only
by economic function, hair in the throat lost in the sea,
the child grows bigger and *and* and *and* and *and* and *and*—

THE LIMITS OF WHAT WE CAN DO

Neutrality is a privilege. The rocks we throw
ourselves onto are a privilege. It is hard to hate
creation on the first day of warmth, but I am vigilant
and a sac still fills up my mother and a sac fills up
my father and a sac deflates my grandmother
and I have no sense of sac. Tory Dent describes
her slow dying as "sham orgasms" and I'm thinking
of expansion, how I read *HIV, Mon Amour* first in the sun on a day
in May with my beach body and my coffee to stay.
I know what I'm doing with this poem is a sham
the way I knew I knew my vivacious privilege
was a portrait of a bad institution; capitalism fingered
my throat with its delicious incentives of eat
and I did eat because I had touched love and love knew what to do
with me. I like poetry because there are no miracles in it;
it is like the dream I had about disease nestled marked
curled as a burst blood vessel in the eyeball, that to own
up to the mark was to look up inside your skull for others to see it.
The poem is doomed and swimming in fluid.
In my dream I wrote an article for *Slate* called "The Limits
of What We Can Do" in the face of annihilation
and it was received well. I wake up nestled marked curled
like clickbait, a deep-sea fishing net. I throw up yarn
and go for a run. A love inside of me is breaking.

ACKNOWLEDGMENTS

Versions of these poems have been published in the following journals. Gratitude to the editors for selecting these works.

The Academy of American Poets Poem-a-Day: "Crescent Moons"

The Adroit Journal: "Psalm for the World Below"

The American Poetry Review: "(Earth), the"

Bennington Review: excerpts from "The Lake"

Black Warrior Review: "Malignant"

BOAAT: "Three of Swords"

The Brooklyn Rail: excerpts from "The Lake"

The Essay Review: excerpts from "The Lake"

The Hopkins Review: "Consultation," "Transverse Orientation"

Hoxie Gorge Review: "Surge," "They Do Not Eat Until They Cleanse Themselves"

Jewish Currents: "There Is Hope"

Mississippi Review: "Imaginal Discs," "The Ritual"

Narrative: "Caliche," "Eat and Keep," "Edge Habitat," "Intercourse"

The Nation: "Natalie Eilbert, by User 4357"

The New Yorker: "The Limits of What We Can Do"

The Paris Review: "Kolumbo, 1650"

PEN Poetry Series: excerpt from "The Lake"

Poetry: "Bacterium," "Mediastinum"

Quarterly West: "The Sun Is Shining"

The Recluse: "Land of Sweet Waters"

Thank you to so many, who have been with me in various stages of these poems and who have given me and my poems a more resilient heartbeat:

Aria Aber, Derrick Austin, Chase Berggrun, Liz Bowen, Amy Brinker, Jamel Brinkley, Orchid Cugini, Chekwube Danladi, Brandon Eilbert, David Eilbert, Grayson Eilbert, Jacqueline Eilbert, Jean Eilbert, Jordan Eilbert, Sarah Fuchs, Marcela Fuentes, Seth Hoffmeister, Claretta Holsey, Hannah Kempf, Jason Koo, Lily Lamboy, Kabel Mishka Ligot, Carrie Lorig, Ricardo Maldonado, Dolan Morgan, Natasha Oladokun, Siena Oristaglio, Allyson Paty, Jessica Roeder, Emily Shetler, Danie Shokoohi, Marlo Starr, Barrett Swanson, Mary Terrier, Rachelle Toarmino, Michael Wiegers, and Kate Wisel.

NOTES

"Kolumbo, 1650" was written in response to the most stunning prompt by poet, interdisciplinary scholar, and bestie Dr. Marlo Starr.

"The Sun Is Shining" takes its title from Richard Feynman's talk "What Is Science?": "All the things that we see that are moving are moving because the sun is shining." He argues it can answer any question on earth, eventually. Presented at the fifteenth annual meeting of the National Science Teachers Association, 1966, in New York City, and first published in *The Physics Teacher* volume 7, issue 6 (September 1969), pages 313–320.

"The Lake" is indebted to the words of many: Matthew Arnold, Mariame Kaba, Alice Notley, Lisa Robertson, George Oppen, Virginia Woolf, Rebecca Solnit, Emily Dickinson, Clarice Lispector, Anne Carson, and Eudora Welty.

"Caliche" is indebted to the frustrating, tremendous saga presented in *Toms River: A Story of Science and Salvation* by Dan Fagin.

"Land of Sweet Waters" takes its title from my hometown of Hauppauge, New York. Hauppauge is Algonquian, and the town boasts that it means "land of sweet waters," but many interpret the term to mean "overflowed land." According to the 2020 US Census, 0.15 percent of Hauppauge's population is Indigenous.

"Consultation" takes its epigraph and inspiration from Megan Fernandes's poem "In Which I Become a Mythology and Also, Executed" from her excellent book *Good Boys* (Tin House, 2020).

"Edge Habitat" came into existence after listening to the poison ivy–themed episode 63 of the podcast *This Podcast Will Kill You.*

The italicized line in "Bone" is from my grandmother Viola Felice's diary.

"Crescent Moons" is dedicated to all survivors of sexual violence.

"Malignant" uses a line from Clarice Lispector's *Água Viva.*

"Psalm for the World Below" uses a sentence from Virgil's *The Aeneid:* "Woman's a thing / Forever fitful and forever changing."

"Chippewa Falls" is for Iliana Peters, who should have been able to turn eleven this year.

"When I said I was moving to Wisconsin . . ." references Julia Wallace in *The New York Times,* 13 February 2017.

"Someone casually says *Earth is menopausal . . .*" references Hiroko Tabuchi, Claire Rigby, and Jeremy White in *The New York Times,* 24 February 2017.

"You're only revising the patriarchal order . . ." quotes Miranda Field's beautiful poem "I Do Not Sleep For Sleep Is Like The Wind And Trees Amazed."

The italicized text from "Last night I sat on a barstool . . ." is from Ariel Dorfman in *The New York Times*, 31 March 2017.

"Great Barrier Reef now . . ." is indebted to a conversation and the poems of Allyson Paty.

Natalie Eilbert is the statewide mental health reporter for USA Today Network–Central Wisconsin. She was a 2021–22 recipient of a National Endowment for the Arts fellowship, and her writing has appeared in *The New Yorker, The Paris Review, Poetry,* and elsewhere. Born and raised in New York, she lives in Wisconsin.

Lannan Literary Selections

For two decades Lannan Foundation has supported the publication and distribution of exceptional literary works. Copper Canyon Press gratefully acknowledges their support.

LANNAN LITERARY SELECTIONS 2023

Jaswinder Bolina, *English as a Second Language*

Natalie Eilbert, *Overland*

Amanda Gunn, *Things I Didn't Do with This Body*

Paisley Rekdal, *West: A Translation*

Michael Wiegers (ed.), *A House Called Tomorrow: Fifty Years of Poetry from Copper Canyon Press*

RECENT LANNAN LITERARY SELECTIONS FROM

COPPER CANYON PRESS

Chris Abani, *Smoking the Bible*

Mark Bibbins, *13th Balloon*

Jericho Brown, *The Tradition*

Victoria Chang, *Obit*

Victoria Chang, *The Trees Witness Everything*

Leila Chatti, *Deluge*

Shangyang Fang, *Burying the Mountain*

Nicholas Goodly, *Black Swim*

June Jordan, *The Essential June Jordan*

Laura Kasischke, *Lightning Falls in Love*

Deborah Landau, *Soft Targets*

Dana Levin, *Now Do You Know Where You Are*

Philip Metres, *Shrapnel Maps*

Paisley Rekdal, *Nightingale*

Natalie Scenters-Zapico, *Lima :: Limón*

Natalie Shapero, *Popular Longing*

Arthur Sze, *The Glass Constellation: New and Collected Poems*

Fernando Valverde, *America* (translated by Carolyn Forché)

Michael Wasson, *Swallowed Light*

Matthew Zapruder, *Father's Day*

Poetry is vital to language and living. Since 1972, Copper Canyon Press has published extraordinary poetry from around the world to engage the imaginations and intellects of readers, writers, booksellers, librarians, teachers, students, and donors.

WE ARE GRATEFUL FOR THE MAJOR SUPPORT PROVIDED BY:

Richard Andrews and Colleen Chartier
Anonymous
Jill Baker and Jeffrey Bishop
Anne and Geoffrey Barker
Donna Bellew
Matthew Bellew
Sarah Bird
Will Blythe
John Branch
Diana Broze
Sarah Cavanaugh
Keith Cowan and Linda Walsh
Stephanie Ellis-Smith and
    Douglas Smith
Mimi Gardner Gates
Gull Industries Inc. on behalf of
    William True
The Trust of Warren A. Gummow
William R. Hearst III
Carolyn and Robert Hedin
David and Jane Hibbard
Bruce S. Kahn
Phil Kovacevich and Eric Wechsler
Lakeside Industries Inc. on behalf of
    Jeanne Marie Lee

Maureen Lee and Mark Busto
Peter Lewis and Johanna Turiano
Ellie Mathews and Carl Youngmann as
    The North Press
Larry Mawby and Lois Bahle
Hank and Liesel Meijer
Jack Nicholson
Petunia Charitable Fund and
    adviser Elizabeth Hebert
Madelyn Pitts
Suzanne Rapp and Mark Hamilton
Adam and Lynn Rauch
Emily and Dan Raymond
Joseph C. Roberts
Jill and Bill Ruckelshaus
Cynthia Sears
Kim and Jeff Seely
Nora Hutton Shepard
D.D. Wigley
Joan F. Woods
Barbara and Charles Wright
In honor of C.D. Wright,
    from Forrest Gander
Caleb Young as C. Young Creative
The dedicated interns and faithful
    volunteers of Copper Canyon Press

TO LEARN MORE ABOUT UNDERWRITING COPPER CANYON PRESS TITLES,
PLEASE CALL 360-385-4925 EXT. 103

The pressmark for Copper Canyon Press suggests
entrance, connection, and interaction
while holding at its center
an attentive, dynamic space for poetry.

This book is set in Banque Gothique and PT Serif.
Book design by Becca Fox Design.
Printed on archival-quality paper.